The
Nature
of
Poetry

Library of Congress Control Number: 2010915145
ISBN: Hardcover   978-1-4535-9428-5
             Softcover   978-1-4535-9427-8
             Ebook   978-1-4535-9429-2

This book was printed in the United States of America.

To order additional copies of this book, contact:

The Nature of Poetry
P.O. Box 721314
Berkley, MI 48072

Contact
natureofpoetry123@gmail.com
To place orders

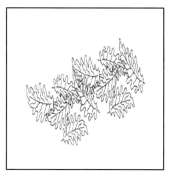

For

Aldo Leopold and Chickadee 65290

immortalized in

Leopold's <u>A Sand County Almanac</u>

and Harry

Acknowledgement

This small book of poetry

commemorates the struggle

to survive breast cancer

and is our small effort

to help find a cure.

Catherine Connelly

Sue Kempinski Hennessey

I know a bank where the wild thyme blows,

Where oxlips and the nodding violet grows,

Quite over-canopied with luscious woodbine,

With sweet musk-roses and with eglantine . . .

~Shakespeare

Table of Contents

Part One

Spring

Liquid Sun

A Monet canvas
painted with pond
shadows.

Maples and poplars
weeping willow boughs lit
with liquid sun.

A great blue heron
crouching statuesque
fishing
on one leg.

Mallards, gulls and Canadas on board
the pond moves
like a baggage carousel.

May Apple Café

Opening for business
green umbrellas
in May apple cafés
promising golden apples.

April Hullabaloo

Mardi Gras morning
golden daffodils
blue jacket hyacinths
saffron crocuses.

Lavender myrtle
clamping trailing stems of
green glossy shoots.

Gossamer Wings

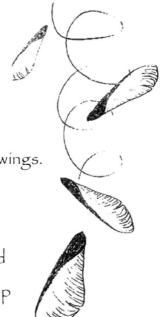

Dangling under maple leaves
clusters of tiny rotor blades
pirouetting down on gossamer wings.

Under foot, fish fly crunch
paisley designs on newly mowed
grass. A spring gust can whip up
a momentary snowstorm.

Wild Carrot Juice

Skunk cabbage as big as rhubarb. In moist
cool grasses, green herons take cover.
Jack-in-the-pulpits showy with green
brocade amulets.

White flat-top florets of
Queen Anne's lace
offer sips of wild
carrot juice.

Boardwalks crisscross cattail marshes
yellow water lilies root deep in
black onyx pools.

Spring Peepers

In scouring rushes
twin fawns take refuge.
Russet deer eat aspen
and tender sassafras shoots.

Marsh marigolds glitter
along an icy stream.
Tiny legions of forget-me-nots
conceal early spring peeper frogs.

As night creeps in
choruses of bantam-sized
peepers chime spring
like tinkling sleigh bells.

Tiffany Lanterns

Slender salmon and
golden Tiffany lanterns,
early columbine
like lightning bugs on
gentle wooded slopes.

Vernal Ritual

Unfurling skunk cabbage
maroon spikes breaking skyward
through crusted March snow.

Hitchhiking Turtles

In moist cool sedges
a sandhill crane
seeks shelter with two
newly fledged chicks.

Wooden planks, weathered
anchored in the marsh,
overlooking
mats of fragrant white water lilies
platforms for hitchhiking
turtles.

Little bobbing balls of velvet
downy signets
floating under a sapphire sky.

A ruby-throated hummingbird
sucking nectar from
cardinal flowers and great blue
lobelia.

Mushroom Woods

Morel mushrooms camouflaged in
last year's leaf litter.
Flowering dogwoods spreading
gracefully like a Japanese still life.

Tulip trees
cats on haunches
begin a new forest.

A pileated woodpecker
tucks its crow-sized body
into a chiseled opening.

Sinewy vines stretch around
ancient trunks tightly wrapping
furry centipede legs.

The Kingfisher Calls

Open water
a pair of Canadas work
the grassy bank
gathering spring sustenance.

Skimming swallows
purple martins
Eastern phoebes
swooping down to grab
mosquitoes on the wing.

Across the ripples
a parchment oak leaf
flutters down sailing.

Mallards glide down on
orange feet
sending out their wake.

The rattling call of the kingfisher
squeaking like rusty bed springs
shooting over the pond
choosing a nearby branch.

Herring gulls soar
ascending then dropping
again and again.

Spring Harbingers

Early wildflowers
white bloodroot
pink hepatica
yellow nodding trout lilies
brighten the forest floor.

A dozen robins illuminate
a dull brown hillside
flickering like Chinese lanterns.

In a staghorn sumac stand
another flock of spring harbingers pick
seeds of burgundy velvet.

Appalachian Majesty

Smokey Mountain haze
layers of
Blue Ridge glory.

Spring hues
pinks, peaches, golds and greens
cover the mountain sides.

White trillium
Virginia blue bells
cut-leaf toothwort
yellow star grass
dot mountain paths.

Silenced Rapture

March blizzards can swirl
snap daffodil necks,
silence purple hyacinth rapture.
Ice coated April can seal
early youth
in crystal tombs.

Part Two

Summer

Slopes of Summer

Summer solstice sun
climbing
bathing forests, meadows
grassy slopes.

Gentle July rains
bathe dry flower stalks
of pink milkweed
wild bergamot
bouncing bet
turning dusty roadsides
bright again.

Black-eyed Susans
yellow St. Johnswort
slopes of summer
glowing with purple fireweed
and loosestrife.

Dappled Sunlight

Trellised ivy gate
scarlet tanager
perched in dappled sunlight.

Pink Sea Salt

Sandpipers on stilts
search for anemones under
pink crystals of sea salt
in tide pools.

Figure Eights

Barn and tree swallows
skim endless figure
eights over summer ponds.

Cattail stalks
protecting blue-winged teals
nesting.
Redwing choruses
fill the marsh.

Abandoned Sneakers

On the old blue dock
abandoned sneakers
in moonlit shadows
against exploding walls of
pale pink rhododendrons.

Garden Party

Today is garden party day
many guests have been invited to
the cobblestone patio
amongst coral bells
purple phlox and pink lamium.

Bumblebees will come.
Goldfinch, English sparrows and chippies
will stop by. Mr. Downy who hammers in
the Quince will be there and
the cardinals four.

Portly pigeons, rambunctious squirrels
and red tail hawks are not
on the invitation list but
they will crash for sure.

Wonderful summer fare:
pink lamium nectar
dill, lavender and sunflower seeds.

Quince apples and rose hips
polished black cosmos seeds for the finches.
Weather permitting
another garden party tomorrow.

Parachute Silk

Money flowers
parachute silk
in bright sunlight—
translucent plates.

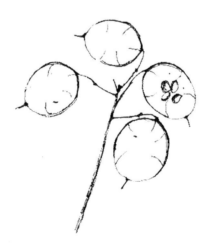

Summer Fanfare

Electric blue indigo bunting
perched
among bursts of Halloween
oriole flourishes.

Flashing Coif

Seeking swirls of currents
male mallard
emerald coif flashing.

The French Market

Pumpernickel wheels
buttery croissants
crisp crusted baguettes.
Blue enamel bowls offering sweet butter
and marmalades. Iron skillets
sputtering with fragrant marinara.

Salads of red cabbage and shredded apple,
chick peas and lentils dressed lightly in
olive oil and lime. Summer squash skins
glistening like polished alabaster.

Brown lacquered beans—
Dominican roast, Kona, Sumatra
cappuccinos and bittersweet espressos.
Rows of sweet syrups—
butterscotch carmel
maple cinnamon
and blackberry cream.

Blueberry and plum flans polished in sweet
veneers. Chocolate mousse
in plump little pots.
Crème Brûlée in torched sugar luster.

Waxing Silver

Silver crescent waxing
atop heavenly perch in
Sistine Chapel blue sky
under lit by rising sun.

Peppermint Satin

Fairytale pink baubles,
peppermint satin
ribbons the corsage.
First love . . .

Part Three

Autumn

Aspen Gold

Mitten weather.
Floating birch leaves
blanketing
the hillside.

Against a lackluster sky
larches
stenciled filigree.

Dry oak leaves curl and crackle.
Fields of goldenrod
chicory
and yarrow delight
meadowlarks.

Bevies of geese congregate on grassy
knolls while hooded mergansers
cruise in full black and white regalia.

Overhead a white egret
black legs outstretched
straight as an arrow
glides down into the cattails.

Gray Flannel Sky

Raven feathers
purple silhouettes against
a gray flannel sky.

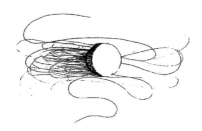

Slivers of Immortality

Silver slivers knitted into
round glowing
moon disk
suspended in
coral washed sky.

Goose Cashmere

Geese scripting V's
long thin skeins of
black cashmere.

Straight as soldier squadrons
marching across the sky
gliding like kite strings.

Safe Slips

Mountain streams
tumble, bubble, polish
glistening boulders. Kayakers
in resilient red plastic
seek safe slips between
rugged shelves of rock.

Peach Moon

Peach-lit
October moon,
sea stars dancing
in the silver mist
on the still lagoon.

Autumnal Equinox

Swarms of blackbirds feed.
Hostas thick with stalks of
white bells. Goldfinches
winter-dressed in olive drab.
A robin's song trilled at sunset
summoning the autumnal equinox.

Kettle of Hawks

Suddenly in the sailing sky
migrating birds.
Kettle of hawks
spiraling
criss-crossing
riding the North Wind.

Ancient Scrolls

Lavender hills of New England asters.
Overhead
a formation of snow geese
gulf coast bound.

Fluttering maple leaves deposit crimson majesty.
Brittle oak leaves rustle
like ancient scrolls.

Tamarack bogs
dull gold
silhouetted lacework
against the autumn sky.

Deer everywhere
sentinels on the paths
grazers in the lowlands
browsers on the slopes.

Waning copper sunrays
filter through
maple and aspen leaves glowing
like dying campfire embers.

Hurricane Lamps

Candlelit coast
under the corn moon
flickering
honey tones
like hurricane lamps.

Part Four

Winter

Frost Laced Window Panes

Frosted glass

glistening ice needles

sparkling

cerulean diamonds.

Crown Jewels

In dew frost

crown jewels

blue quartz and violet blush.

Cathedral Glass

Snow flowers
iceberg green
cathedral glass
caught in the frozen sea.

Snow Shoeing

Traversing
pristine snowfields—
stands of pines
cattail spikes
framing water holes.

Up and down
following gentle curves
of summer fairways
blanketed with
diamond chips
twinkling blue in the
blazing sun.

Trails ribboning
doubling back.
Rawhide lacing
stretched taut, echoing
the ancient Ojibwa.

Stamped waffles in the snow.

Snowshoes

pressing stars

glistening

like cutout cookies.

Sparrow Lace

Tiny sparrow feet
dancing love lace
on the fresh snow.

Winter Residents

Cardinal red

black chickadee caps,

flashing white

junco tails

lighting up a drab thicket.

White Pine Royal Guard

Magical snow puffs

transform

winter woods

capping tree stumps with mushroom hats.

Dots of snow cotton

turn graceful young beeches into

spring pussy willow

groves.

Winter pastry cooks

dust rows

of white pine soldiers

with bags of confectionery sugar—

awaiting

the allusive sun's

liquid silver to fasten

diamond festooned jackets

on the royal guard.

Lace Caps

Snowflakes

drifting

catching

red dogwood berries.

Fastening

snow collars on

lace capped hydrangeas.

Part Five

Shadows of Winter

Swan Wings

Bathed in copper afterglow

pewter poplars

casting long

snow shadows.

Twinkling star fields,

ice shards weighing down

weeping willows.

Lilac shadows

dancing on frosted ferns

beneath sea clouds of

swan wings.

Amethyst Ice

Beneath the slate sky

cirrus wisps of

silver threads

drift past the winter sun

bathing glazed woodland snow

in forest shadows on

amethyst ice.

Rose Twilight

Queen Anne's lace

tattered and stoic

in forest shadows.

Upland snow caps

glacier blue in rose twilight.

Forest Dance

Ice ballet

danced on

twilight shadows of

drifting snow.

Part Six

Halloween Sparrow

The events in this poem actually occurred
during the fall of 2007.

Halloween Sparrow

What happened?
How did the bird get in?
Through capped chimney screen
and glass fireplace doors ajar, perhaps.

A dead English sparrow
in the dining room
on its back
little feet curled.

A shiny crow
in midnight black
like a dead stiff cat
might have gotten an even louder cackle
than this supine sparrow.

This was Halloween
the night of ghouls and goblins
howling graveyard winds
eerie shrieks and
a rigid little bird.

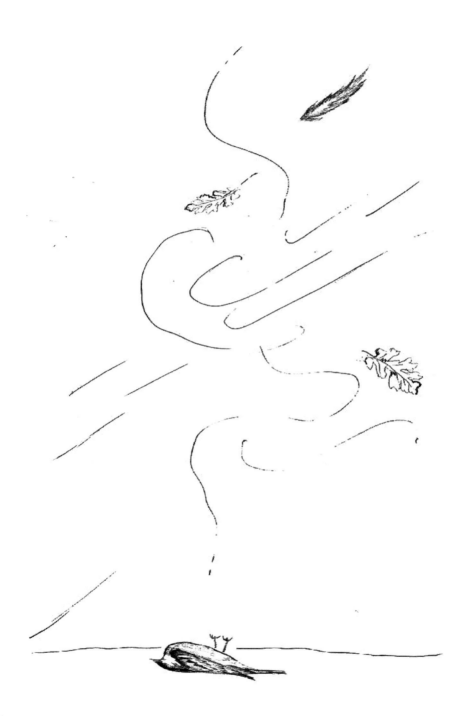

Soon ghosts and wart-nosed witches

scarecrows and skeletons

golden winged angels

and pirates in red and black bandanas

would be at the door.

I scooped up the little carcass

positioned him gently in

Kleenex in a shoebox

and laid a bright fuchsia geranium.

I placed the little cardboard casket outside

on the edge of the patio

hoping for a quick completion to life's cycle.

Carrion, a possibility on this night of nights.

Who would take the little casualty?

The bossy neighborhood jay

an opportunistic o'possum

cranky Mrs. Murphy's Tom cat?

Maybe even a bold hawk

brave to venture so near.

Daily

I checked the box

monitoring the cool fall temperatures

replenishing the flower.

But the little corpse remained.

I was relieved

no eyes pecked out

or ragged incision

exposing an empty heart cavity.

Surprised the body still remained

whole, lying in state.

After almost three weeks of coffin tending

on the Saturday before Thanksgiving

an empty tomb.

The little feathered occupant gone.

I discarded the make-shift casket

relieved the sparrow

had finally departed.

What happened next was as totally unexpected

as unwarranted.

Not five minutes passed
after discarding the cardboard box.
Suddenly there was a furious aerial attack
launched high from the backyard maple.

Rain drops pelted me.
Black ink ran down the kitchen window.
Inky blobs stained the patio.
I looked up and saw fifty to eighty blackbirds
stenciled
dark against the blue sky
letting their inky, runny streams fly
as if on cue.

The assault was perfectly orchestrated,
splattering my hair and white sweatshirt.
It was synchronized, premeditated and
launched in unison.

The birds were chattering
defiant
like a pack of teens.
I was frantically waving my hands
then hurling spent quince
at the top of the tree.

Finally, the flock departed
leaving the stained landscape
marked indelibly with a message
for me to decipher.

Was the Halloween casualty
one of their own?
Had I usurped primordial power? Intruded into
ancient aviary burial customs?
What was the prehistoric ritual
I had betrayed
to deserve such wrath?

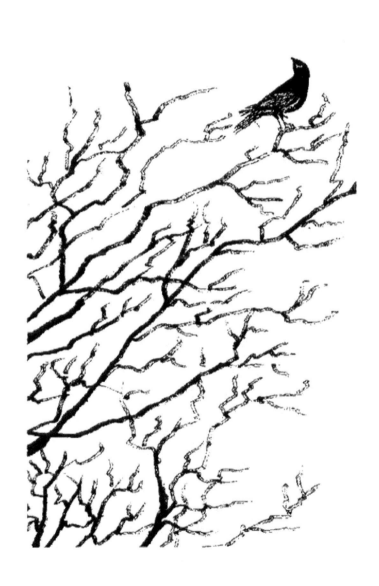

About the author

Catherine Connelly's life was shaped by her journeys growing up as an army brat in the U.S. and Sweden. Known as an avid birdwatcher, environmentalist and Master Gardener; summers are spent planting, tending, and harvesting hundreds of pounds of vegetables for local soup kitchens. As an enthusiastic hiker she has come to know native flora and fauna, enjoying the beauty and wonder of each season.

About the illustrator

Sue Kempinski Hennessey has been in the field of art for over 40 years working in many different mediums. Her dear friend and still mentor, Catherine Connelly, has given purpose to her life by choosing and giving her the freedom to do these illustrations. The front cover design has two meanings; with one celebrating the tenacity of life and the other as a pen quill and ink well as the writer and illustrator begin filling this book with nature's greatest gifts.

Front Cover Illustration:

Skunk Cabbage, symplocarpus foetidus

Quill and Ink

Your support in Breast Cancer Awareness
brings us closer to The Cure.

For additional purchases of

The Nature of Poetry

Contact Xlibris publishing at

Toll Free 1-888-795-4274 to order by phone

Or

www.Xlibris.com/bookstore the online bookstore.

Visit

Amazon.com

Barnes & Noble.com

Correspondence may be made by writing:

The Nature of Poetry

P.O. Box 721314

Berkley, Michigan 48072